THE EVOLUTION OF HOME

THE EVOLUTION OF HOME

ENGLISH INTERIORS
FOR A NEW ERA

SIMS HILDITCH

Emma Sims-Hilditch with Giles Kime

FOREWORD BY KIT KEMP
PHOTOGRAPHY BY SIMON BROWN

New York · Paris · London · Milan

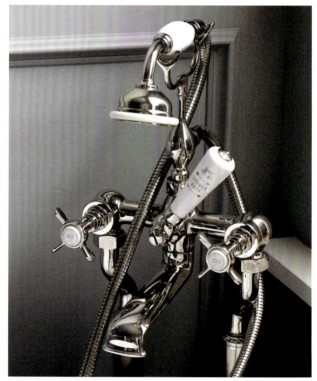

Contents

FOREWORD by Kit Kemp 7
INTRODUCTION 9
FEATURED PROJECTS: CITY & COUNTRY 10

1. Making an Entrance 21
2. Relaxing 47
3. Cooking 83
4. Eating 103
5. Bathing 133
6. Sleeping 163
7. Working 209
8. Organizing & Maintaining 223

SIMS HILDITCH DESIGN STUDIO 241
ACKNOWLEDGMENTS 255

Foreword

BY KIT KEMP

I got to know lovely Emma Sims-Hilditch over the course of a number of years. She has an engaging character *and* elegance. Most of all, she is very good at what she does.

Emma and I agreed early on that English style means different things to different people. For some, it might be the intimate interior of a thatched cottage; for others, the drawing room of a manor house in the Cotswolds. Whatever one's interpretation, it's less about a look and more about the creation of a pleasing, relaxed atmosphere.

For the two of us, English style is most interesting when it is evolving. It owes perhaps its greatest transformation to Nancy Lancaster and John Fowler, who succeeded in bringing an extraordinary freshness and clarity to a look that was in their time overburdened with past formality. Since then, a succession of designers—from David Hicks and Chester Jones to Nina Campbell and Ben Pentreath—has played their part to further change and lighten the style, particularly by using color and interesting textiles and materials.

More recently, I have been interested in the work of those who have taken a pared-back approach in order to create a look that combines the elegant feel of classic English houses with a more contemporary take on the practicalities of daily life. Some of the best examples of this style are the interiors conjured by Emma, who has been unwavering in her focus on employing classic good looks, comfort, and functionality to create outstanding homes. Emma establishes a pragmatic foundation on which she builds the most pleasing interiors that relate to the character of the architecture and place.

As someone who has spent some years designing hotels and residences both in London and New York, I find Emma's approach to her craft is one that resonates strongly. Interior design should be about anticipating the needs of the people who occupy a space: clients, guests, diners, and staff. The ambition should be to create rooms that satisfy all the senses and foster comfort and well-being.

Of course, color, pattern, texture, and soulful pieces—both old and new—play their parts, too. Emma's ability to bring all the required elements into perfect harmony is a balancing act I admire very much.

OPPOSITE An outbuilding in the garden of The White Hart, the sixteenth-century former coaching inn near Bath where the Sims Hilditch team is based. The roughly hewn limestone is typical of the area.

Introduction

OPPOSITE Emma was photographed early in her career for the June 2005 issue of *House & Garden* (*lower left*). She originally based her business at a former schoolhouse in Wiltshire, a picturesque county about eighty miles west of London, where she and her husband, John (*upper left and center right, with Emma*), brought up their two daughters, Daisy and Betty (*upper right*), and son, Billy (*lower right*). Emma, who enjoys sharing her knowledge about design, has hosted events with the coauthor of this book, Giles Kime (*pictured with Emma, on bicycles, center left*).

Many designers learn their trade at college or in the studios of other designers. For me, it was working on film sets while I was in my twenties, and then spending thirty years creating an ever-evolving home in Wiltshire with my husband, John. Creating beautiful, perfectly functioning spaces—whether for family or clients—has required an equal mix of inspiration and experience. Designing sets for film director Ridley Scott didn't just teach me how important it is to always look at the bigger picture, it also made me realize that without planning and attention to detail, it's almost impossible to make the most of creative ideas. On its own, style is never enough.

It was while I was working in the film industry that I met and fell in love with John, then a young officer in the army. We married and soon afterward he left the army and cofounded Neptune with Giles Redman. The enterprise, which produces furnishings for the home and garden, has been an important part of my creative journey. Early on, there was no option for me but to generate an income while bringing up three small children. Starting with making curtains at the kitchen table, I eventually graduated to full-scale interior-design projects. A turning point was a commission to design an entire nine-bedroom Grade II–listed manor house. Over the same period, the former schoolhouse where we started our married life (and still live today) evolved to suit our changing needs, first to meet those of our three children—Daisy, Betty, and Billy—and then those of my fledgling business, which has now spread its wings and found a new perch in a nearby coaching inn we converted.

A major phase in the evolution of our home was converting an adjoining barn, which hugely tested our combined skills. It required us to think laterally in order to add a kitchen and sitting room on the ground floor, and our own bedroom up in the eaves. What we learned was that when creating spaces, you can achieve almost anything with planning and imagination. It also taught us that at the heart of every successful home is a series of practical, carefully conceived rooms that enhance the quality of daily life.

As the house evolved, so did my business. With each of the succession of projects—which has ranged from country residences to London town houses—came exciting new possibilities. Yet the challenge has always been the same: to create homes that make people feel happy, spaces to relax in with family and friends. So far, that has been a very satisfying and gratifying experience.

Featured Projects: City & Country

Throughout this book you'll see images of some of the residences we have worked on over the years, from barn conversions to grand houses. Many are listed, which means that they have been identified as being of historic significance and protected as a result. Our past projects are in locations as disparate as seaside villages and fashionable London districts. However, wherever we work, and whatever type of house, our approach is always the same: to collaborate with our clients in the creation of stylish, comfortable homes that offer the perfect settings for everyday life, from relaxing and entertaining to cooking and working.

A GEORGIAN TOWN HOUSE IN CHELSEA

While many of the houses we are asked to transform are in the countryside, we are increasingly asked to work on residences in cities, particularly in London and Bath. This house is in Chelsea, one of my favorite parts of London, on the banks of the River Thames. The area has an artistic past: both Turner and Whistler lived and worked in the neighborhood, and you can still see artists' studios on Tite Street and Mulberry Walk. The owners of this town house also own the lakeside house in Surrey we worked on (*see page 17*), and they were keen for a sophisticated feel with many bespoke touches. With this in mind, we used a palette of deep blue and emerald green, accented with dark wood floors, textured linens, and soft velvets. Like many town houses, it has a basement with limited natural light, a reality that we embraced with cabinetry in deep, inky colors that are contrasted with pale limestone flooring.

Whenever possible, Emma and her team take a holistic approach. They address all aspects of a project, including the relationship between indoor and outdoor spaces, such as this terrace of a London town house.

A VICTORIAN TERRACE HOUSE IN PARSONS GREEN

If you travel west along London's King's Road (until 1830 it was a private thoroughfare, originally reserved for Charles II's trips to Kew), you will eventually reach Parsons Green, a residential district dominated by Victorian houses. John and I recently bought a terraced house in the area; we stay there when we need to be in London, and my team at Sims Hilditch uses it as a base for client meetings. It also serves as a showcase for our work and, with this in mind, we were keen to push the boundaries with a complete architectural transformation. Ceiling heights were raised throughout and rooms were designed with meticulous detail, including state-of-the-art technology and en suite bathrooms. Downstairs, a cinema room leads to a courtyard garden.

The garden, designed as an extension of the interior, is perfect for entertaining in the warmer months.

A SEASIDE COTTAGE IN CORNWALL

One of my favorite parts of the world is the rugged coast of Cornwall, which my family and I have explored over the years in our boat. Over time, we decided to establish a base in St. Mawes, a small fishing village on the Roseland Peninsula, for family holidays and as a rental property. Our plan for the interiors of this house was not just to make them comfortable and relaxing, but also to make the most of the spectacular views, the light, and the beautiful garden. As much as possible, we worked with natural materials such as stone, wood, and linen, which are complemented by a palette of crisp whites and soft grays.

Perched on a rolling English hillside, the house was designed to make the most of the beautiful coastal views beyond.

FEATURED PROJECTS: CITY & COUNTRY

AN ANCESTRAL HOME IN NORTH YORKSHIRE

This historic house sits at the center of a sporting estate in a beautiful, far-flung corner of the British Isles, and it has been in our client's family for more than five hundred years. The interior had changed very little since the early 1900s, and bringing it back to life was a wonderful project to lead. The nine-bedroom house had been updated incrementally during the Georgian and Victorian eras, and we worked with listed-building specialists to sympathetically restore the architectural features of the structure, including the chimneypieces and original stone flooring. We also restored much of the antique furniture and introduced a color palette inspired by the surrounding countryside. The result is a historic house that is fully equipped for twenty-first-century living.

An avenue of beech trees leads to the historic house that Emma and her team brought back to life.

A FORMER SCHOOLHOUSE IN OXFORDSHIRE

This beautiful house on a thousand acres in Oxfordshire had been derelict for decades when we began the design journey. Our initial focus was on the house's layout and the flow between spaces. We created a large, open-plan kitchen with simple steel windows and a passage to the garden, where our clients keep ducks and chickens and grow fruits and vegetables. Decoratively, the goal was to create a family-friendly house rich in bold colors and pretty fabrics.

Standard bay trees punctuate the front elevation of the building, lending it a distinctly Provençal feel.

FEATURED PROJECTS: CITY & COUNTRY

A REGENCY TOWN HOUSE IN BATH

There are few cities with more charm or history than Bath, in Somerset. Famous since Roman times for its hot springs, Bath became a popular spa town during the Georgian era, when many of its famous buildings were constructed, most notably the Royal Crescent, Pump Room, and Circus. Bath is also close to our offices in the small country village of Cold Ashton. We were delighted to be tasked with the sympathetic transformation of this Regency town house, which is typical of its era. The house is Grade I listed, and we were keen to enhance its unique atmosphere with classic pieces that we sourced for the project. Nevertheless, we also wanted to make it a comfortable home; with that in mind, we incorporated a number of contemporary touches, such as bespoke joinery that harmonizes with the original design.

The jewel-like colors of two original Georgian stained-glass windows are in marked contrast to the muted palette of the interior.

A LAKESIDE HOUSE IN SURREY

This is a classic Sims Hilditch project, where we combined the best of traditional and contemporary living in a comfortable family home that also offers sophisticated spaces for entertaining. As with all our projects, a great deal of planning went into the layout; here, the focus included dedicated areas where children can study and play. Another important element was bespoke cabinetry, which provides the storage that is so vital for a busy family.

This Grade II–listed house has been reconfigured so that modern luxuries, including a swimming pool, complement its classic charm.

A CONVERTED BARN IN WILTSHIRE

This is our family home in pretty Wiltshire, where my husband and I raised Daisy, Betty, and Billy and where I started my interior-design business. While it has evolved over the years, the most transformative change was our purchase of an adjoining barn, which allowed us to add a sitting room with a mezzanine level and dramatically high ceilings. Throughout, we worked with Cotswold stone and timber in warm colors to create a look and feel that is true to the barn's agricultural roots.

Multilevel landscaping lends an integrated appearance to the cluster of buildings, which have been joined to create an extensive family home.

A CONTEMPORARY TOWN HOUSE IN KNIGHTSBRIDGE

Our team prides itself on versatility; while we have a signature style, we will always flex it in whichever direction we believe will lead to the most successful outcome. This house in the leafy London district of Knightsbridge was one of our most contemporary projects. We added fully bespoke cabinetry and furniture, custom de Gournay wallpaper, and a wine cellar, as well as introduced a color palette of watery blues, grays, silvers, and taupe, with bolder shades in the kitchen and snug (a cozy seating area).

The calm interior creates a sanctuary in the center of the city. The scheme for the sitting room includes a cornice that acts as a pelmet.

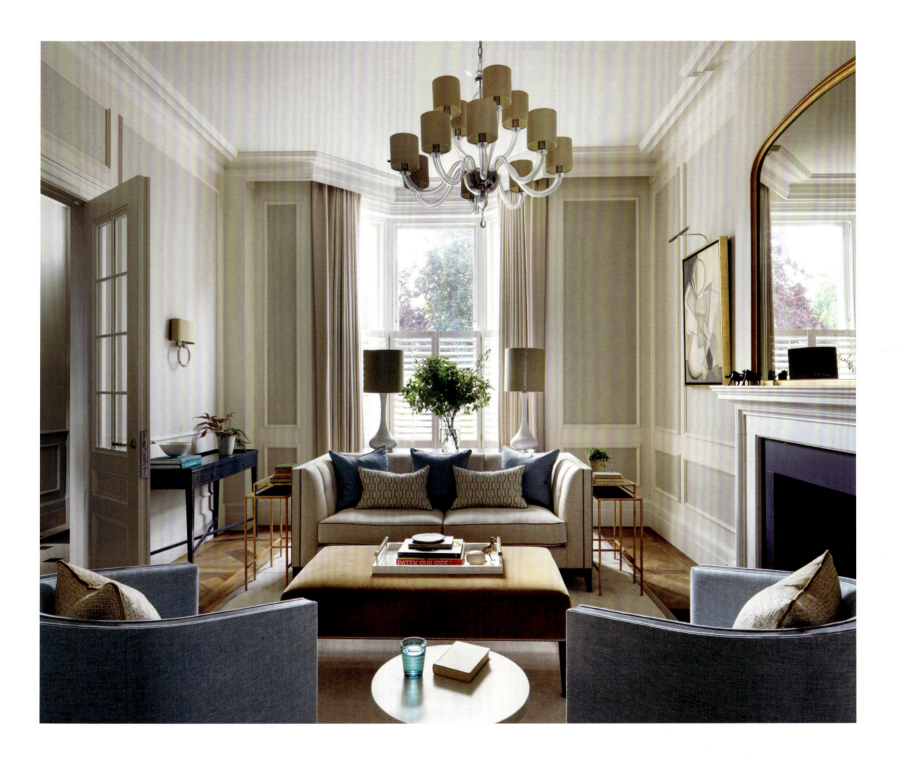

1. Making an Entrance

Whatever the size of an entrance hall, it is a place that offers many exciting opportunities for design. The entry in larger houses is often a double-height space where you can play with scale; a large pendant light can achieve further drama. So, too, can large items of furniture such as a striking console, longcase clock, hall table, or artwork that lends focus, draws the eye, and sets the scene for what's to follow.

Yet even in smaller country properties and town houses, an entrance is where we make visitors feel welcome. A deeper paint color or large-scale wallpaper can both lend intimacy and warmth *and* provide a great backdrop to collections of paintings and photographs. Fresh flowers always transform a space and, along with scented candles, offer an inviting treat for the senses. Few entries, however large, have much natural light, so we use lamps and wall lights to create atmosphere. Consider any opportunities to maximize light; even small wells and windows admit natural illumination that will bring the space to life.

When choosing a wall color, consider how it will relate to those in nearby rooms, such as a sitting room, study, or kitchen. The tonality of the colors you choose is key to ensuring a smooth transition from one space to another.

Function is important, too. In large houses, where there may be mudrooms and laundry rooms adjacent to the kitchen, the main entrance may be more ceremonial. Conversely, in smaller houses—particularly those where there are young children—it may be necessary to ensure that a vestibule works harder with the help of storage and shelves recessed in alcoves. In either case, it's important to plan how the spaces will work: where will you keep keys, mail, sports gear, and children's school bags? The more organized the spaces, the more effortless it will be to arrive and leave.

Because an entrance hall is a busy space with a lot of foot traffic, think carefully about floor material. A robust, hardwearing surface is vital, and one that can be combined with underfloor heating will negate the need for radiators, which is a significant boon if space is tight.

However you decorate an entry, ensure that it not only is well planned but also reflects the mood of the rest of the house; it is a visitor's initial experience of a home, and we all know that first impressions count.

AN ANCESTRAL HOME IN NORTH YORKSHIRE

OPPOSITE The wealth of architectural detail in the house's main entrance hall—which includes an ornate door lintel and a beautiful cabochon floor that combines limestone with black insets—was added gradually as the house evolved in the eighteenth and nineteenth centuries. ABOVE Compared to the main entrance hall, the secondary stair hall is a simpler but still elegant space.

RIGHT In transforming the house, Emma and her team have retained the spirit of this much-loved family home that dates back more than five hundred years. The focus of the family's daily life is the magnificent double-height entrance hall, which was constructed as part of the transformation of the house to connect two neighboring buildings. As well as an entrance, it serves as an informal entertaining space in a relaxed and welcoming environment that sets the tone for the whole house. The symmetry imposed by the arrangement of furniture, hunting trophies, and ancestral portraits creates a coherent feel that echoes architectural features such as the arches and galleried landings.

OVERLEAF The project involved seamlessly mixing new furnishings with the client's existing pieces, all set against a muted color palette. The pared-back arrangement of furniture not only makes for a calm, curated feel that is in keeping with the heritage of the house, but also is ideal for the demands of twenty-first-century living and prepares it for generations to come.

ABOVE A damask-style wallpaper by Totty Lowther and carefully configured arrangements of furniture have been used to create intimacy on the upper level of this imposing space. A wide range of lights, including table lamps and mirrored sconces, offers versatile lighting options. OPPOSITE An oversize brass lantern from Jamb is a dramatic addition and fills the space beneath the vast glazed cupola.

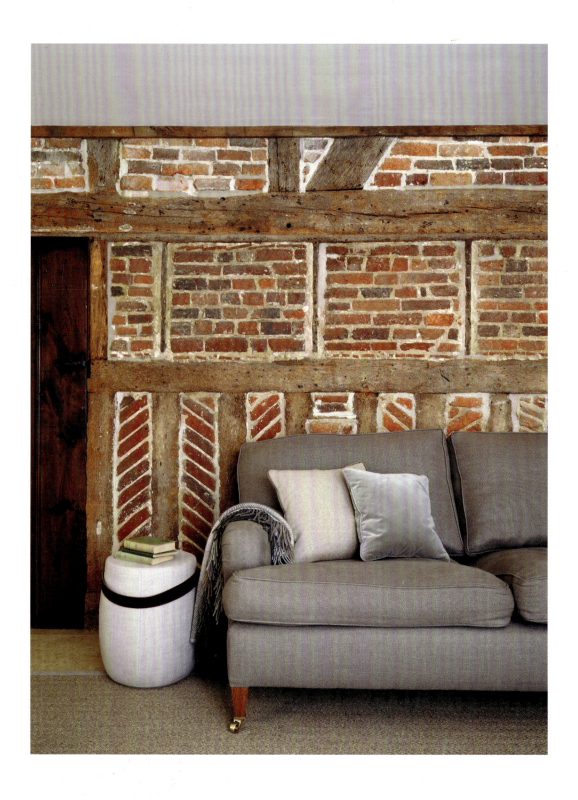

A LAKESIDE HOUSE IN SURREY

ABOVE Crisp upholstery in linen and velvets contrasts with the texture of exposed brickwork.
RIGHT Paring back the structure to expose the beams not only adds texture but also creates an open feel in what would otherwise have been a confined space. A palette of rich colors, along with woolen upholstery and pleated lampshades, complements the mood of the interior.
OVERLEAF A wide inglenook fireplace imbues the house with period charm.

A CONVERTED BARN IN WILTSHIRE

ABOVE A mixture of limestone and timber not only reflects the rural setting of the house but also is a practical combination in high-traffic areas. **OPPOSITE** A large mirror, resting on the console table, and bold paintwork bring light and color to the period interior. The table offers discreet boot storage.

A SEASIDE COTTAGE IN CORNWALL

OPPOSITE Even the smallest entrances can offer opportunities for extra storage, in this case shelving that has been inset into a wall. **ABOVE** An oak console table provides useful space for table lamps, vases, and storage baskets. Simple paneling creates a coherent feel. Rattan furniture and wooden lamp bases give a relaxed feel and add texture.

A FORMER SCHOOLHOUSE IN OXFORDSHIRE

OPPOSITE This elegant space is also extremely practical, offering room for coats, a seat for changing footwear, and ample storage. A large steel lantern lends drama. **ABOVE** An under-stairs space has been fitted with carefully planned, bespoke cabinetry that offers useful additional storage for outdoor clothing.

MAKING AN ENTRANCE

A CONTEMPORARY TOWN HOUSE IN KNIGHTSBRIDGE

ABOVE There are many ways to enhance the feeling of spaciousness in a period building. Here, a pair of glazed doors creates the impression of space and allows light to pass from one area to another.
OPPOSITE An elegant, contemporary console makes the most of the limited space.

A REGENCY TOWN HOUSE IN BATH

ABOVE The combination of a tufted-leather antique chair and a bar with a mirrored counter creates a welcoming impression, and the cabochon floor complements the classic look of the marble bust displayed in the niche. **OPPOSITE** The impressive architectural detail of the room is enhanced by a striped stair runner, which adds subtle pattern, and a distressed mirror panel visually expands the space.

ABOVE The Regency interior displays plenty of distinctive architectural details, such as stained-glass windows and decorative metalwork on the stairs, as well as fine antiques. **OPPOSITE** A console with a pair of colored-glass lamps makes for a pleasing, symmetrical arrangement that is ideal in a hallway.

2. Relaxing

The joy of a sitting room is that it offers an opportunity to spend time with family and friends without any distractions. Comfort, of course, is the focus, and it's worth seeking out the best-quality sofas and armchairs the budget affords. Yet, to me, comfort is about so much more than upholstered seating; it relies on an interplay of lots of different factors, including lighting, color, texture, and a collection of furniture and objects that make you and your guests feel at home.

As a starting point, I like to decide what role the room will play in a client's life. While most people's idea of a sitting room is a rather grand space, today's sitting rooms tend to be much less formal than a generation ago. It remains, however, a place for relaxation, in addition to one that encourages conversation.

A sitting room is a great place to mix antiques, art, and fabrics that are perhaps a little more indulgent than those used in rooms that are enjoyed on a more regular basis. Architectural detailing such as paneling, cornicing, and decorative plasterwork is also important here, and when planning a new house, these embellishments can be key elements in the design of a sitting room, used to add an extra layer of visual interest. The symmetry of a distinctive fireplace is a great foundation on which to build. The other important ingredient of a scheme that needs careful thought is seating, such as sofas, armchairs, and slipper chairs. Also consider club fenders that are a useful source of additional seating when you are entertaining a crowd. I love to center furniture on a large, button-tufted ottoman with reeded legs and brass casters. Like an upholstered fender, this piece of furniture will also offer an opportunity to add a striking or luxurious fabric.

A scale plan sketched on graph paper will not only allow you to make the most of the space, but will also prompt you to consider how people will relate to one another, and to other significant features such as a fireplace, while in the room. Some people view this process as a way to ensure that items of furniture "talk to one another." Plan a spot within reasonable reach of each seat where a cup or glass can be set down (adding a large tray to an ottoman increases your options).

This stage of the planning process should also involve lighting—furniture placement and sources of light should go hand in glove, and thinking ahead will allow you to locate wall or floor sockets to avoid meandering electrical cords. A wide range of lighting options is important and should include a mix of table and floor lamps (all on the same circuit so they can collectively be adjusted via a dimmer on a light switch by the door), some pretty wall sconces, and perhaps an antique chandelier. Picture lights also play their part, giving paintings the attention they deserve while also creating warm pools of light during the evening.

Creating an atmosphere is such an intangible subject that many people shy away from addressing it when planning a scheme, yet it is vital. It's important to create a sitting room with a distinctive feel that is removed from the rest of the house. While dimmable lighting is an important consideration, there are many other additions that can conjure different moods and appeal to the senses, from fragrance diffusers (Dr. Vranjes Firenze is a particular favorite) to a Sonos sound system. Texture is important, too, so I like to use velvets, wools, and natural linens; wool throws not only add texture but also protect upholstery from small children and four-legged friends, while patterned upholstery is more forgiving of stains.

Carefully chosen furnishings and collections of objects—antique furniture, sculpture, paintings, and decorative accessories—set the mood brilliantly (many of my clients like to include a baby grand piano, which creates a festive feel even when it's not being played). Invest in at least one piece of furniture that will create a significant *wow* factor, such as a striking console or armoire. It will become a captivating focus that can't fail to draw the eye. You can achieve a sense of place with works of art depicting the local landscape.

In a sitting room, I love to use feather-and-down upholstery because it has that extra layer of luxury, especially in the seat cushions of a beautifully handmade sofa. The latter might not be quite so practical for everyday use, but when the room gets used less often, it feels so special to sink into a full feather-and-down armchair or sofa. In smaller, more intimate rooms, such as a TV room that is used on a daily basis, sofas and armchairs with feather-and-foam seat cushions are a practical option because they retain their shape. Durable upholstery fabrics are also a smarter choice in spaces that are used regularly.

The colors you choose for walls, curtains, and blinds will also impact the mood. For example, in south-facing rooms, deeper hues will balance the bleaching effect of strong sunlight. Don't be tempted to use very pale colors in north-facing rooms—they can look very cold. Richer hues work well in small, intimate rooms that are mainly used in the evening.

While comfort is important, it isn't by any means the only factor to consider in a sitting room, TV room, or den. It is just as important that these rooms reflect your own tastes and, more than anything else, make you, your family, and your guests feel at home.

AN ANCESTRAL HOME IN NORTH YORKSHIRE

OPPOSITE Panels of a hand-painted de Gournay wallpaper lend an elegant and decorative feel to this formal drawing room with impressive proportions. **OVERLEAF** Upholstery and cushions in a mix of soft colors including pale green, pink, blue, and yellow combine to create a layered yet cohesive look and serve to update a room that comprises elaborate period architectural detail.

OPPOSITE A collection of treasured antiques including ceramics, silver, and a set of three decanters (known as a tantalus) is displayed against a rich, yellow ocher. **ABOVE** Curtains and a large rug complement the richness of the walls to create a solid foundation for this scheme. A sofa, a pair of armchairs, a large upholstered ottoman, and scatter cushions are covered in windowpane checks, florals, plush velvets, and heathery linen that combine to give a cosseting feel to the informal sitting room.

A REGENCY TOWN HOUSE IN BATH

RIGHT The classic look of this room, with its high ceiling, original plaster ceiling rose, ornate pelmet, carved fire surround, and club fender, has been updated with upholstery in a mix of textured wovens in a muted, contemporary palette as well as bespoke shelving. Together, these elements meld to create an elegant but comfortable space.
OVERLEAF This multi-functional but extremely elegant space makes effective use of the open floor plan of the house. The discreet kitchen is well away from the side-by-side dining and living areas, which have a luxurious look with fine textiles set against a backdrop of distressed mirror.

A CONTEMPORARY TOWN HOUSE IN KNIGHTSBRIDGE

ABOVE This smart sitting room has an elegant art deco feel that offers the owners a sanctuary away from life in a busy city. At the window, louvered shutters offer both light and privacy. The sofa is flanked by a pair of elegant table lamps that create a calming symmetry. **OPPOSITE** The space is dominated by a pair of abstract paintings, which adds interest, manipulates proportions, and enhances the tonal color scheme.

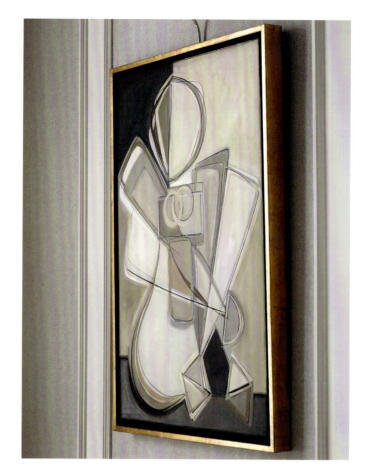

OPPOSITE Elegant materials and finishes add interest and definition to the luxurious sitting room.
ABOVE This cinema room was arranged on two levels to create a theater-style assembly of seating. The bold colors of the acoustic wall covering contrast with the similarly striking red upholstery of the two chairs in the foreground. Simple ottomans and occasional tables offer places for drinks and snacks during screenings.

A VICTORIAN TERRACE HOUSE IN PARSONS GREEN

The transformation of this classic Victorian town house included the removal of some internal walls and installation of glazed steel screens. Here, a velvet sofa in soft blue is set against a backdrop of neutral shades.

RELAXING

LEFT This relaxed basement den leads directly to a terrace at the rear of the house. Deep red walls conjure a cosseting feel. The room, which doubles as a home cinema, has a screen that can be lowered from the ceiling and an overhead sound system. **ABOVE** Wooden paneling creates the warm feel of an alpine chalet.

A GEORGIAN TOWN HOUSE IN CHELSEA

OPPOSITE This is a good example of how Emma and her team distill the essentials of a large, elegant sitting room into a space that is smaller but no less perfect. The scheme relies on a deep bottle green—seen on the ottoman, lampshades, cushions, and cabinetry—to create a striking and highly sophisticated room. **ABOVE** The cornicing above the window also doubles as a pelmet.

ABOVE This room—which is used for relaxing, reading, and watching movies—has fitted cabinetry that makes the most of the limited space, with storage not just for books and games but also for the television. At the far end, a drinks table is a welcoming destination. **OPPOSITE** Details such as brass handles, inlays, and fringed trims create a luxurious finish.

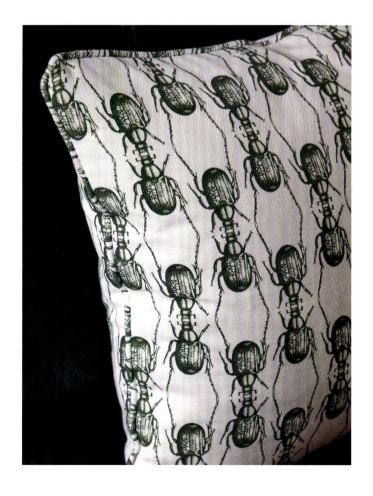

A FORMER SCHOOLHOUSE IN OXFORDSHIRE

OPPOSITE Rather than designing storage that blends in with the walls, Emma and her team often prefer to make a statement by choosing to paint cabinetry in bold, striking colors. In this room, the combination of a convex mirror and a simple stone fire surround creates a focus while the large ottoman softens the appearance of the space. **ABOVE** Paneling with boards of irregular widths also adds interest.

A SEASIDE COTTAGE IN CORNWALL

ABOVE When this space was planned, the intention was not only that it should be pleasing and comfortable but also that it shouldn't distract from the beauty of the sea views. **OPPOSITE** Pale linen upholstery, cushions in a variety of fabrics, and muted colors create a look that is perfectly in tune with the beautiful setting of the house.

A LAKESIDE HOUSE IN SURREY

OPPOSITE This relaxed sitting room and dining space make the most of the beautiful surroundings. **ABOVE** A clever use of space and comfortable furniture has ensured that the comfort of the house hasn't been compromised by its historic roots. **OVERLEAF** Upholstery with studded detailing and a collection of artwork create a distinctive look in a sitting room.

A CONVERTED BARN IN WILTSHIRE

ABOVE When restoring their Wiltshire schoolhouse, Emma and her husband were keen to reveal as much of the structure as they could. When specifying new materials, they selected options with texture such as shiplap boarding and stone floors, which provided a mixture of both warmth and character. **RIGHT** Having lived in the house for many years, they eventually had the opportunity to incorporate an adjoining barn, creating a double-height space with a sitting room below and a bedroom on a mezzanine above. The lofty bookcase makes the most of all the available space. **OVERLEAF** Textured walls lend a rustic feel and contrast with the clean lines of the stone fireplace.

3. Cooking

We wholeheartedly buy into the idea that "you are what you eat," with the result that we have chosen to follow a mostly plant-based diet, which we feel is kinder to ourselves and to the planet. That decision guides not only what we eat but also the way we plan spaces, with kitchen gardens close to the main house so that they are always front of mind and easy to access. Even having herbs in a window box offers a way to engage with growing food, and it's also a vital way of teaching children about where food comes from.

For me, the kitchen is the living, breathing center of the home, and creating the perfect design is about achieving a balance between beauty and functionality. After decades of planning kitchens, I discovered that there is no reason why these two qualities should be mutually exclusive. We have also discovered, through many happy years of sailing, that a lack of space needn't be an issue either. You learn a great deal when cooking dinners for eight in a small galley kitchen, in particular how to make the best use of every inch of space. And careful planning is just as important in large kitchens, where the distances between the different elements can be quite substantial; in that case, it's essential to effectively create a "kitchen within a kitchen," with ingredients that are used on a regular basis close to the cooking and food preparation areas, and the rest in the pantry or secondary kitchen.

When space allows, an island is a perfect option. A kitchen island has its roots in the "cook's table," the workhorse of large Victorian and Edwardian country-house kitchens, which can still be seen in National Trust properties. In its twenty-first-century incarnation, the kitchen island provides extremely space-efficient storage as well as a place to prepare food, cook, and enjoy casual meals. Islands have a sociable feel that allows everyone to get involved in cooking or simply to enjoy a glass of wine while keeping company with the cook. When creating a dedicated cooking zone in a large kitchen, an island offers an ideal opportunity to establish a divide between the cooking area and the eating area. If incorporating a dishwasher, it's important to position it on the side of the island that faces the dining area—behind paneled doors—so that dishes can easily be cleared away after a meal.

Glass-fronted, wall-mounted cabinets are ideal for storing glasses and mugs that are used on a regular basis, and it's always useful to have oils, vinegars, herbs, and spices within easy reach of the stove. Also, consider dedicating a standalone, larder-style cabinet for breakfast items such as plates, bowls, mugs, a kettle, and a coffee maker—if you have to leave in a rush, it is better to have the option of closing the doors than to leave a mess! I tend to prefer having more drawers rather than more cabinets, because it's easier to organize drawers than cabinets and finding things in them is much quicker.

The great advantage of painted work surfaces in the kitchen is that they can be refreshed on a regular basis. However, I also love wooden and Carrara-marble work surfaces. Wood is also great for kitchen flooring, because it has more give than stone and concrete, and so is much easier on a cook's back and feet when standing for long periods of time. We like to include as many natural materials as possible in a kitchen, including wood, stone, and terracotta; they help to create a softer look than the industrial style of some kitchens, and they also age beautifully.

I use the same approach to decorating a kitchen that I use for any other room. I often hang paintings or a mirror with a distressed finish on the wall behind a stove. They add interest and personality to the space—as, of course, does antique furniture such as cupboards and dressers that inject color and texture as well as provide useful extra storage.

A SEASIDE COTTAGE IN CORNWALL

OPPOSITE Natural light and a garden view make this a pleasing environment in which to prepare food. Incorporating seating in even the most limited space creates a sociable feel.

A CONTEMPORARY TOWN HOUSE IN KNIGHTSBRIDGE

OPPOSITE Floor-to-ceiling cabinetry makes the most of all the available space. Choosing a bold color for cabinetry lends a dramatic feel to a kitchen; here, it is a striking contrast to the white work surfaces.
ABOVE Beyond the dining table, glass doors leading to a terrace flood the space with natural light. Parquet floors create a sleek, contemporary feel.

OPPOSITE A freestanding hutch in a warm neutral shade creates a contrast with the darker color of the cabinetry (across the room) and offers plenty of storage for china and glass that is conveniently close to the dining table. **ABOVE** Wine storage can easily be incorporated in otherwise dead spaces. Glazed cabinetry has a lighter feel and makes it easy to locate stored items.

A FORMER SCHOOLHOUSE IN OXFORDSHIRE

RIGHT The combination of simple paneling comprising boards of uneven widths and steel-framed doors creates a crisp, industrial feel. A more capacious alternative to an armchair, the love seat offers the perfect place to relax. The upholstery adds a splash of vibrant color.
OVERLEAF The cabinetry has a mix of painted and unpainted surfaces, and the countertop's pale color maximizes all the available light. Limiting the amount of wall-mounted storage creates an open feel.

A CONVERTED BARN IN WILTSHIRE

White cabinetry is set against gray walls, creating a fresh feel. The boarded ceiling lends a warm, rustic look. Shaded overhead lights offer effective task lighting.

A LAKESIDE HOUSE IN SURREY

This kitchen has been treated with what is known as a color drench, which involves painting both walls and cabinetry in the same color. Here the look is lightened—and given a glamorous edge—with a mirrored backsplash behind the Rangemaster.

AN ANCESTRAL HOME IN NORTH YORKSHIRE

LEFT The glorious main kitchen, illuminated by a skylight, includes cabinetry and furniture in five different colors, creating a lighthearted, slightly whimsical feel. The central island provides a preparation area that is ideal when large events are being catered. **ABOVE** This simple ancillary space retains its period feel with stone floors and traditional furniture and is used for social lunches.

COOKING 97

A GEORGIAN TOWN HOUSE IN CHELSEA

ABOVE A combination of a deep blue finish and richly colored wood creates a dramatic feel that is perfect for casual entertaining. **RIGHT** The mirror behind the Wolf cooker, as well as light from the distinctive pair of glass lanterns over the table, helps to make the most of the limited natural light in this basement space. Artwork on the walls and the two niches on the left-hand side of the Wolf add depth and detail that elevate the space above being purely functional.

OPPOSITE Brass details add a classic glamour to lighting, cabinetry, and the sink. **ABOVE** Open shelves lend added interest to the space, with an extensive collection of glassware and barware as well as wine storage and a small sink, creating dedicated space for making cocktails and serving drinks. A marble surface is the ultimate luxury in any kitchen, even if it is only in one area. On the rear wall is a sheet of mirror that enhances the feeling of space and light in the kitchen.

4. Eating

Food is the lifeblood of our lives—growing, cooking, and of course enjoying it with family and friends. While on a day-to-day basis we often eat and entertain in our kitchen, there's nothing we love more than a dedicated dining space. A dining room—or simply even a space adjacent to the kitchen that has its own look and feel—can have a cozy atmosphere and, when styled for entertaining, can become quite magical. When guests have made the effort to dress up, a space with a bit of glamour can summon a memorable ambience, particularly when there is something to celebrate. Key to this is lighting, which is an important part of creating mood in any room. In addition to a range of lighting options—all on dimmers—picture lights that illuminate artwork create a wonderful feel.

Of course, you can also add drama with the paint, wallpaper, and fabrics you choose. Curtains and upholstered chairs enhance the mood and have the practical benefit of absorbing sound, which is really useful if there are lots of people gathered together. While it's quite an investment, I love to cover dining-room walls with fabric; it achieves a quiet, cosseting feel *and* it's very practical, as fabric is much more robust and forgiving than paint or wallpaper.

Decor that is personal to you, such as a collection of art that you've acquired over the years, will give the room a look that is all your own. We love to display the work of our daughters: Daisy, a painter, and Betty, who works in set design but who also paints between projects. Daisy's landscape paintings create a wonderful sense of place, particularly those of the Cornish coastline and the Swiss Alps, both of which we know well. I also love to include paneling, which lends formality and allows you to manipulate proportions. One of my favorite types is waist-high paneling—or wainscoting, as it is sometimes known—which I like to paint in a color different from the walls. Antique furniture offers another way to add mood. Side tables and corner cupboards provide useful storage for all the paraphernalia of dressing up a table, from napkins and tablecloths to cruets and candlesticks.

Of course, not all houses have dining rooms. Even open-plan kitchens, however, offer an opportunity to add a touch of drama to the space where you are entertaining. In addition to careful space planning that will maximize views and avoid high-traffic areas, well-devised lighting will offer significant benefits. Pendant lamps and spotlights, on independent dimmer switches, will provide both task lighting for cooking and versatile mood lighting for relaxing and entertaining. When lights in the kitchen are dimmed, it will throw the focus of attention on to the dining area. An island will help to create a physical divide between the cooking area of the kitchen and the dining area.

Terraces also make great dining rooms. I treat outdoor entertaining the same way I do entertaining inside—the goal in either location is to create a distinct feel. As well as carefully planned hard landscaping, I use topiary pots to demarcate the space and then add lighting to create atmosphere. Otherwise the principles are just the same: comfortable furniture, as well as great table linens and accessories, will create a wonderfully decorative and relaxed place to entertain. I like to concoct a showstopping tablescape using patterned china with flowers and greenery from the garden. If you have the opportunity to build a new terrace, siting it off the kitchen to ensure easy access is very useful; alternatively, if you have a pool house with kitchen amenities, consider setting up the outdoor dining space nearby.

A CONVERTED BARN IN WILTSHIRE

OPPOSITE A second dining area is adjacent to the main kitchen area and offers garden views during the day and a more intimate feel in the evening. The low-maintenance garden is planted with box and lavender, which add simple shapes and structure.

LEFT This room is illuminated by a large skylight that floods it with diffuse light throughout the year. The mixture of materials—exposed Cotswold stone, shiplap boards, and stone floors—brings warmth and texture to the space, as do oak tables and woven chairs. **ABOVE** The terrace, with its dry stone walls and garden beyond, offers the perfect backdrop to outdoor entertaining.

ABOVE Low-maintenance furniture with robust surfaces is the ideal option for outdoor spaces.
OPPOSITE An open-sided agricultural building such as a cart shed offers the perfect setting for relaxed outdoor entertaining; in summer the large area of roof offers shade and protection from occasional showers, while in cooler months a firepit will take the edge off freezing temperatures.

A VICTORIAN TERRACE HOUSE IN PARSONS GREEN

ABOVE A wall-mounted bench seat makes the most of all the available space and provides storage beneath. On the rear wall, paneling of irregular widths creates a relaxed backdrop. The space is lit by a skylight. **OPPOSITE** With the steel-framed doors open, the kitchen is seamlessly joined to the garden. The absence of wall-hung cabinets enhances the feeling of space.

A FORMER SCHOOLHOUSE IN OXFORDSHIRE

ABOVE A row of wall-mounted lights creates an intimate feel in the evening and, when illuminated, helps to distinguish the dining area from the rest of the open-plan space. **RIGHT** On the wall is the "Jungle Birds" design by English designer Marthe Armitage. Cushions in different patterns add a discrete mix of colors.

A LAKESIDE HOUSE IN SURREY

RIGHT A magnificent mahogany table lends a formal feel to this dining room. Large casement windows, which offer multiple views of the outdoors, bathe the space in light.
OVERLEAF Discreet pattern and metallic touches create a decorative look in this room. The wealth of architectural detail is given a coherent feel with the use of just one color. A range of lighting options—including a pair of table lamps, an ornate pendant, and a picture light over the painting—creates various moods for dining and entertaining.

AN ANCESTRAL HOME IN NORTH YORKSHIRE

LEFT Rather than choosing a more classic option for the walls of a large country-house dining room—such as a Pompeiian-red paint, damask-style wallpaper, or flock—Emma and her team selected a more contemporary color that places the room firmly in the twenty-first century and also offers a crisp contrast to the elaborate architectural detail, such as the pedimented doors. A large, edged sisal rug adds another contemporary touch to the space. Together they create a pared-back setting that allows the client's furniture and ancestral portraits to look their best. The floral curtains at the windows add richness and warm colors into the mix.
OVERLEAF The wealth of materials and decorative objects—both new and old—creates a layered look. Ancestral pieces and portraits lend a wonderfully personal atmosphere.

EATING 119

OPPOSITE The project was a great example of how designers can transform a house while working with its existing antiques and family portraits. **ABOVE** A striking arrangement of picture window and fireplace creates the focal point for this breakfast room. A painted cupboard, table lamp, and floral curtains inject lively color.

EATING

A REGENCY TOWN HOUSE IN BATH

ABOVE This ground-floor kitchen, fitted with contemporary cabinetry, leads to a terrace that offers the perfect space for outdoor entertaining as well as panoramic views of Bath beyond.
OPPOSITE The dining space is flooded with light from floor-to-ceiling windows. A large panel of pieced smoked mirror on an adjacent wall adds a sophisticated touch.

A CONTEMPORARY TOWN HOUSE IN KNIGHTSBRIDGE

In this elegant and symmetrically arranged dining room, a paisley-style woven adds a luxurious touch to the backs of the chairs.

OPPOSITE Dedicated storage for wine not only makes good use of dead space but also is more accessible than a cellar and more secure than outbuildings. This was the work of the Sims Hilditch team, who planned carefully configured, temperature-controlled racks at a specified angle with sliding shelves. **ABOVE** Glazed doors make finding and identifying wine easier. **OVERLEAF** With both a dining table and sitting area, this garden is perfect for entertaining. Behind the woven garden fence panel is a shed for storage.

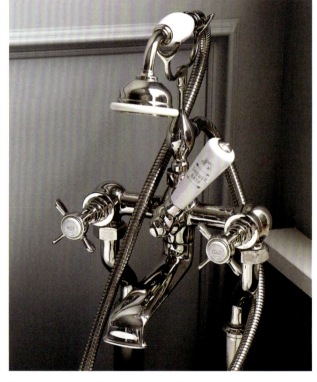

5. Bathing

For most of us the bathroom is one of the ultimate sanctuaries, secluded from the rest of the house. To create a sumptuous atmosphere, it's important that it doesn't feel too clinical. Just as I decorate any other room in the house, I consider every last detail in the bathroom. There's no reason why, if space allows, one shouldn't include small items of upholstered furniture, antiques, patterned rugs, wall lights, chandeliers, prints, paintings, and wallpaper, all of which will elevate the space to a private retreat where you will want to spend time relaxing. If you opt for a freestanding bathtub, consider painting it a striking color that will give the room a distinctive look. If possible, also explore the idea of positioning the bathtub to have an interesting view.

Lack of space should never be a problem when planning a luxurious bathroom, and the ability to squeeze the smallest shower room next to a bedroom can be transformative, especially when planning guest accommodations. Ideally, I like to split bathrooms and shower rooms into two separate spaces. Configuring the various elements—bath, sink, toilet, and shower—can feel like attempting to solve a Rubik's Cube, but it is also extremely satisfying when you eventually arrive at the solution.

We try to avoid being faced with the toilet when you open the door, but otherwise there are very few rules. I often streamline the look by boxing in the water tank, either by setting it into the wall or turning it into a useful shelf. A wall-hung toilet always makes the space seem larger and makes cleaning so much easier. Remember the little details, such as a hook on the back of the door for hanging a dressing gown.

Where possible, try to make a bathroom feel as cozy as possible; I like to add fielded wainscot paneling halfway up the wall or tongue-and-groove paneling if you want a simpler, more rustic look. People tend to use far more tiles than they need; you require only enough above bathtubs and sinks to protect the walls from water. For the countertops, wood makes a great alternative surface to ceramic or stone. A large sheet of mirror fitted behind the bath or sink will also expand the feeling of space significantly. In addition to a heated towel rail that doubles as a radiator, underfloor heating helps create a wonderfully comforting feel.

Storage is key to making the most of a space; a custom washstand should offer all the space you need, especially when paired with a mirrored cabinet. If you need more, however, wall-mounted cabinets and shelves will provide plenty of room for storage without using much-needed floor space.

As in any room, including a variety of lighting options will pay dividends. Lights on either side of a mirror create a much more flattering glow than lighting over the mirror. Also, we recommend a dimmable light that will allow a variety of options—from a soft light that is ideal for a long soak to much brighter light that is required for cleaning.

If the bathroom is en suite rather than standalone, remember to plan the paint colors and surfaces in tandem with the adjoining bedroom so they work together. For a hotel-style touch, you may consider fitting the bathtub in the bedroom, which creates the opportunity to chat—or just to enjoy a beautiful view—from the comfort of your bath.

A CONTEMPORARY TOWN HOUSE IN KNIGHTSBRIDGE

OPPOSITE A Chinese-style de Gournay wallpaper lends a classic look to this luxurious bathroom. A simple braid adds a sleek, tailored look to the Roman blinds. On the walls, wainscot paneling offers an effective way to inject an architectural feel to a scheme.

A pair of sinks flanks the bathtub in this stylish bathroom. Luxurious materials include the cabinetry with metal inlay as well as marble wainscotting, countertops, and floors.

A GEORGIAN TOWN HOUSE IN CHELSEA

LEFT A simple voile blind creates privacy while filling the space with a soft, diffuse light.
ABOVE A marble top adds a luxurious touch to a double vanity unit. **OVERLEAF** Inlaid details, marble mosaic, wainscot paneling, a glass table, and louvered shutters give this bathroom a crisp, cleanly defined look.

A VICTORIAN TERRACE HOUSE IN PARSONS GREEN

ABOVE A simple shelf provides a home for three landscapes by Emma's daughter Daisy, adding a personal touch to the intimate space. Where possible, a niche is always a useful feature in a bathroom for soap and shampoo. **OPPOSITE** The main bedroom has an adjoining bathroom furnished with a double vanity in oak with a marble top. Steel-framed glass panels and doors make the most of all the available light, and a curtain provides privacy when required.

A REGENCY TOWN HOUSE IN BATH

OPPOSITE A decorative panel at the window creates a focus for this room and, together with a voile panel, offers privacy when required. **ABOVE** The bedroom suite includes this dressing room, which is centered around an island that provides both storage and a place to pack luggage. Additional closet space is behind doors that are glazed or mirrored.

AN ANCESTRAL HOME IN NORTH YORKSHIRE

ABOVE This simple scheme includes a wealth of architectural detail. With the addition of a nursing chair, prints, and wall lights, it has all the comfort of a sitting room. **OPPOSITE** Decorative details add an important layer to this bathroom and contribute to its pleasing atmosphere (*clockwise from upper left*): wall lights have a classic feel; goblet headings add a smart, tailored detail to curtains in a simple, small-scale print; ornate bathtub feet add gravitas; and on the steel-and-glass table a variety of objects not associated with bathrooms add interest to the space, including a stack of books and a small glass vase.

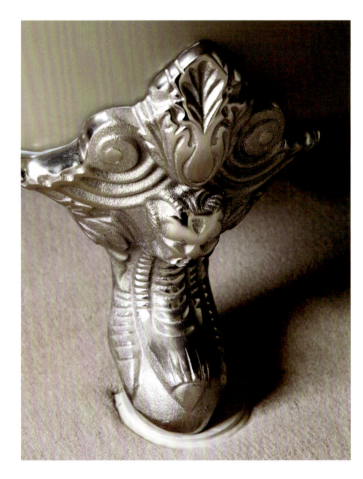

The existing architecture of this bathroom has been allowed to speak for itself. The large marble-topped basin complements the paneling while the freestanding bathtub and pedestal table are sympathetic to the look and feel of the space.

ABOVE The charm of this powder room is derived from the beautiful Lewis & Wood wallpaper. Artist Andrew Davidson featured the client's house in the engravings on which the paper was based.
RIGHT Two shades of yellow complement the floral curtains and botanical prints as well as offer the perfect counterpoint to the rich color of the elegant mahogany table at the window.

ABOVE Bespoke cabinetwork, designed by Emma and her team following antique precedents, houses the toilet and lends this bathroom a traditional feel, complemented by a fern wallpaper and an Edwardian-style washbasin. OPPOSITE A combination of drawers, open shelves, and hanging space allows for ease in locating items, when compared to dressing rooms fitted with cupboards.

A FORMER SCHOOLHOUSE IN OXFORDSHIRE

OPPOSITE The herringbone-patterned floor tile lends texture to this simple shower room. An inset niche within the shower enclosure is a useful feature. **ABOVE** Paneling, patterned blinds, and a vanity unit with louvered doors lend distinctive character to this pretty bathroom.

A SEASIDE COTTAGE IN CORNWALL

In this simple scheme, a floor inset with pebbles adds a textural feature to the crisp, Mediterranean feel created by the white woodwork, tiles, and louvered shutters.

A CONVERTED BARN IN WILTSHIRE

The freestanding bathtub was sourced from a reclamation yard by Emma. She repurposed it by painting the exterior and legs in Pigeon by Farrow & Ball.

A LAKESIDE HOUSE IN SURREY

ABOVE Victorian-style taps add a classic feel to this bathroom. **RIGHT** The colors of the paint, the blinds, and the marble tiles combine to create a cohesive and restful theme. **OVERLEAF** A deeply tufted chair, floral wallpaper, and full-length curtains add to the feeling of comfort in this luxurious bathroom. The toilet is hidden behind the door in the corner of the room for privacy.

6. Sleeping

A bedroom is a sanctuary for me—a calm, clutter-free, organized, and comfortable space in which to relax and reenergize. Ideally, it would have a view down a leafy street, across the sweeping countryside, or over the most pleasing aspect of a garden.

Along with a well-positioned bed, the foundation of any successful bedroom is efficient storage. Before planning anything else, it's essential to calculate which clothing will be in regular use. The rest should either be given away or consigned to long-term storage. At this stage, it's also important to assess whether you'll have additional storage in a dressing room or bathroom, both of which will allow the bedroom to be a restful space devoted solely to sleeping. If you are reconfiguring the layout of the house, remember that if bedrooms are well planned, they don't have to be large. In some instances you might decide to sacrifice an additional bedroom to create a dressing room.

Having planned the position of the bed and storage, the next step is to carefully consider additional elements such as an ottoman, small armchair, and a desk or console that can double as a dressing table. A tall mirror is also important, not just for dressing but also as a brilliant way to bounce light around the room.

I love to introduce architectural detail, particularly if original details have been lost. We upgraded all the cornices in our London residence, which enhanced the space with a discreet classical element. Deep baseboards and door architraves will have the same effect. To further enhance the architectural feel, consider adding striking wallpaper or a rough-board ceiling; there's also a wide range of paneling choices, from raised-and-fielded to Shaker and tongue-and-groove, that are reminiscent of the domestic areas in historic country houses. Whichever option you choose, it will add warmth and interest that is harder to achieve with a plain plastered wall.

We added working gas fireplaces to bedrooms in a number of our London projects, which creates such a cozy atmosphere. In the country, consider installing a woodburning stove that, combined with a basket of logs, lends a wonderfully rustic feel.

Soft neutrals and watery shades have a soothing effect; however, if you are keen for a darker hue, botanical greens will make a room feel restful and nurturing. In a north-facing bedroom, there's a danger that white will feel cold and unwelcoming, so opt for a warmer color with greater depth. For a calm and restful bedroom, consider painting all surfaces, including the walls, ceilings, and woodwork in a single color. If a room has a high ceiling with a cornice, painting both the same color will make the ceiling seem lower; conversely, painting the walls and cornice the same color, and painting the ceiling in a different hue, will have the opposite effect and make the ceiling seem higher. If you prefer wallpaper, a paper-backed linen wallpaper gives small rooms extra detail and a luxurious, cocooning feel.

When planning a small bedroom, it's tempting to think you must have a small double bed. In fact, it's often better to choose the largest possible size and turn it into a feature by adding an overscale headboard in a bold pattern. Alternatively, opt for a plain linen headboard paired with patterned cushions. A valance offers another way to add color and pattern.

If space allows, I always place a chest of drawers beside the bed. In this context, symmetry is less important than people think; an antique chest of drawers on one side looks good when partnered with a table on the other. I always try to include at least one item of antique "brown" furniture and carefully chosen artwork that lends importance to a space. Playing with scale will also make a statement; for example, large lamps by the bed can't fail to create a distinctive feel.

Bedroom lighting requires much more than just a pair of bedside lamps. In my view, a variety of light sources is important: downlights for cleaning and packing; decorative lighting such as pendants, wall lights, and table lamps; and bedside mini LED reading lights that are invaluable for nighttime reading.

Timber flooring is a great option for bedrooms, and in our bedroom in London we have combined it with underfloor heating and a soft wool rug, which sits half under the bed. I feel this combination offers the perfect balance and adds wonderful character to any home, particularly in the city.

Over the years, we have always been huge fans of natural flooring for bedrooms in our own residences and in our projects. Sisal comes in many different patterns and colors and gives a house huge amounts of character and charm; it's important to note, however, that it's not particularly practical for those with pets or young children because stains are virtually impossible to remove. More recently, we have been using ribbed carpets or synthetic flooring, which looks like sisal and is hugely practical. Antique carpets also lend a wonderfully distinctive feel.

Sometimes, we like to create hotel-style touches, such as large-statement headboards, which can create a wonderfully luxurious feel and offer a real sense of escapism.

A REGENCY TOWN HOUSE IN BATH

OPPOSITE The striking sylvan wallpaper creates the impression that this bedroom is borne aloft in the trees and sets the mood for a peaceful scheme that comprises a palette of soft, neutral tones.
OVERLEAF In the master bedroom, a simple design of trailing white flowers on a gold background by de Gournay sets a similarly soothing mood. An antique walnut chest and gold floor lamp blend effortlessly into the mix.

A CONTEMPORARY TOWN HOUSE IN KNIGHTSBRIDGE

ABOVE In this bedroom, a simple armchair in a striking teal fabric takes its cue from the painting over the fireplace and sets the tone for the space. **OPPOSITE** The pared-back shapes of the furniture create a discreet art deco mood. The four-poster bed is a good example of how large-scale furniture can be used to conjure a more intimate feel in rooms with lofty ceilings.

ABOVE A large mirror fitted with a pair of wall lights provides a discreet setting for a dressing table. **OPPOSITE** A wide range of cupboards and drawers designed by the Sims Hilditch team provides ample storage for a couple. **OVERLEAF** This child's bedroom has a crisp color scheme—enlivened with a deep red—and alcove storage that combine to create a sophisticated look that won't need updating in the teenage years.

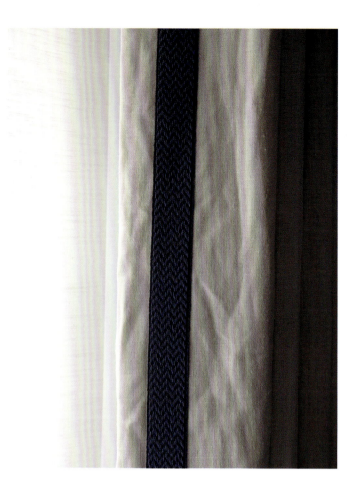
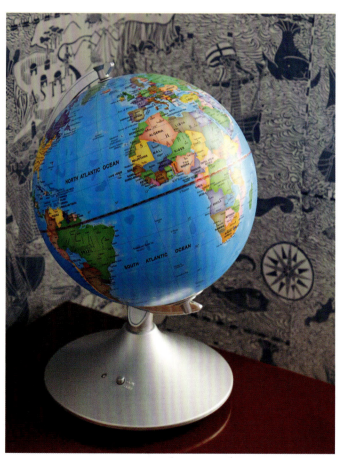

A GEORGIAN TOWN HOUSE IN CHELSEA

ABOVE The gentle curves of an elegant headboard set the tone for this bedroom suite. Fringed edging on cushions, stud detailing in the headboard, and high-quality linens combine to create a luxurious feel. **OPPOSITE** At the window, a curtain with a soft pelmet is paired with a Roman blind. A handsome antique chest elevates the mood.

Inlaid brass detail and linen panels add a neatly tailored look to this custom cupboard and demonstrate the infinite possibilities of bespoke craftsmanship.

ABOVE Despite the challenging proportions of this room in the eaves of the house, it has been artfully designed as a comfortable bedroom with a simple built-in dressing table and adequate storage. **OPPOSITE** The large-scale wallpaper distracts the eye from the sloping walls. A tufted headboard and fringed cushions create a comfortable, layered look.

ABOVE Nailed upholstery, fringed throws, printed linens, and decorative trims are details that contribute to the highly sophisticated look. **OPPOSITE** This built-in bed is an example of how good design and bespoke cabinetry can create solutions that are elegantly space efficient. A cupboard, open shelves, and a bed with storage below have all been included along one wall.

A VICTORIAN TERRACE HOUSE IN PARSONS GREEN

This room eloquently demonstrates the functional and aesthetic benefits of pelmets; they cover the curtain track and add a touch of sophistication. When well-made and properly lined, curtains are thermally efficient. Here, a wallpaper in a colorful, large-scale pattern is offset by neutral fabrics on the headboard, bench, and curtains.

ABOVE When space allows, a large bedside table offers useful extra space for clothes storage.
OPPOSITE Although it's in London, this bedroom has the rustic feel of an alpine chalet thanks to paneled walls, exposed rafters, a knitted throw on the bed, and a textural carpet. The mustard-yellow curtains and cushions add warmth to the otherwise neutral scheme.

A CONVERTED BARN IN WILTSHIRE

OPPOSITE When Emma and John incorporated an adjacent barn into their Wiltshire farmhouse, they created this master bedroom on the mezzanine level. Rustic paneling and lightweight linen curtains create a relaxed feel. **ABOVE** Wood and natural flooring lend the space warmth and rusticity.

A FORMER SCHOOLHOUSE IN OXFORDSHIRE

OPPOSITE The space between two cupboards has been transformed into a bespoke dressing table with storage, providing an efficient solution in a small bedroom. **ABOVE** A steely-gray tufted headboard and a French-style bedside table lend a stylish feel to the cozy room.

ABOVE The subtle pattern of a two-color wallpaper creates a soothing backdrop to this tranquil space. The choice of Roman blinds (rather than curtains) at the window frees up space for a dressing table.
OPPOSITE The bed has an elegant headboard in the same fabric as the blinds, with stud detailing around its outer edge. A bedside table and a table lamp in a mirrored finish create a discreetly luxurious look.

ABOVE Two large-scale polka-dot cushions and a striped bed skirt add a whimsical touch to this bedroom. **OPPOSITE** This small bedroom for a child is a great example of Emma and her team's highly practical approach to working in a confined space. The area between the end of the bunk and the window has been transformed into seating and storage in a corner that might otherwise have been wasted space.

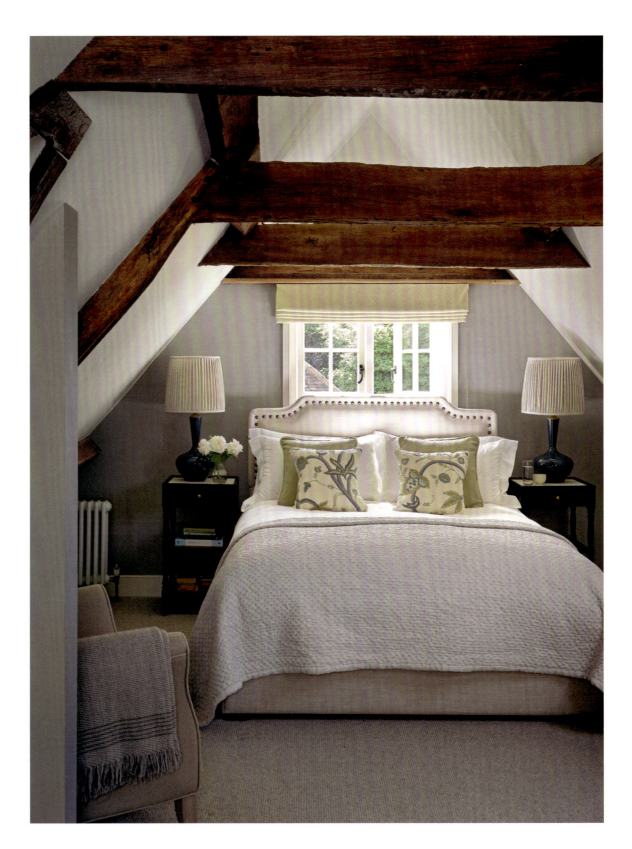

A LAKESIDE HOUSE IN SURREY

LEFT Upholstered furniture is a great addition to a bedroom, not just as a place to sit but also somewhere to leave clothes. Even the most modestly proportioned room can be zoned for sleeping, reading, and dressing. **ABOVE** The challenge with working on a period building is making sense of awkward spaces. For this bedroom, Emma and her team employed symmetry and careful space planning to achieve both comfort and a tranquil beauty.

SLEEPING 195

ABOVE A pair of quirky works of art helps to emphasize the symmetry in this child's bedroom.
OPPOSITE Clever design and bespoke woodwork combine to accommodate a bunk bed with underbed storage, a desk, and plenty of bookshelves in a child's bedroom. The striking choice of color creates a lively feel.

A SEASIDE COTTAGE IN CORNWALL

LEFT The decor of this bedroom is kept deliberately muted so that it doesn't distract from the breathtaking scenery. **ABOVE** The location of this house, overlooking the harbor at St. Mawes, makes it a perfect setting for a marine theme. The yacht wallpaper is an appropriate choice and is complemented by the crisp blue and white chosen for the bed. Here, shutters offer a space-efficient alternative to curtains. **OVERLEAF** A blue-and-white wallpaper in a floral pattern is a great match for the bold stripes of the blanket. In another bedroom, the bed has a pair of bolsters in an ikat design, and above is a set of prints featuring nautical flags.

AN ANCESTRAL HOME IN NORTH YORKSHIRE

OPPOSITE In this bedroom suite, a coherent color scheme ensures that the adjoining rooms work together. The trailing floral of the wallpaper has a scale that is perfect for a large room with high ceilings. **ABOVE** A mixture of plain and patterned cushions gives the scheme a focus while the subtle pattern on the sofa creates a layered look.

OPPOSITE A soft-pink stripe brings warmth to this traditional scheme. **ABOVE** In the corner is a chair in a simple damask-style print. **OVERLEAF** The classic country-house decor reflects the verdant surroundings and artfully weaves together a floral textile, mahogany furniture, and a palette of soft greens.

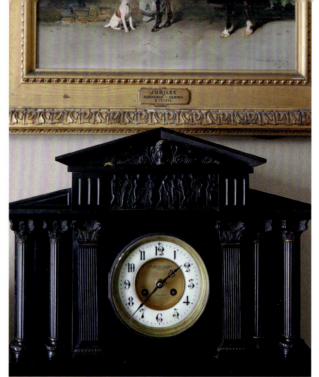

7. Working

With the advent of wireless technology, it has never been easier to work almost anywhere that suits your purposes, so creating a space at home where you can operate efficiently and comfortably is of paramount importance. For me, a home office can be anything from a cupboard with a slide-out desk where you keep your files, to a standalone building in the garden. In between, there can be everything from a desk in the corner of the kitchen or on a landing to more traditional home offices or studies. There's no doubt that, if space allows, a dedicated room away from the action is a significant asset.

Wherever you choose to work, the fundamentals remain the same—the environment must be not only ergonomically efficient, but also pleasing. Increasingly, our clients prefer a home office to feel more like a sitting room than a study, with paintings, curtains, and upholstered furniture. As in any other sitting room, we set out to create a mood, with a mix of rich colors and dimmable lights, that puts people at ease (let's not pretend that there aren't times when work can be stressful). If you pursue the sitting-room option, remember that the chair at which you will be seated for a long period of time needs to be designed for that purpose, rather than one made for sitting at a dining table.

If you have an outbuilding that can be converted, or sufficient space to build a new structure, a standalone home office is a great long-term investment. It's a real benefit (both practically and psychologically) to be able to put some physical distance between home and work, as well as to be able to shut the door at the end of the day. If you decide to go this route, consider creating a space that combines some other purpose, such as a guest accommodation, a gym, or a yoga room. At our design studio, The White Hart, we converted a former coaching inn into a purpose-built studio for my interior-design team. We also converted an old garage into an outdoor studio that gives no hint of its past life.

Whatever the style of the space, ensure that you make the most of any natural light; a desk by a window allows for illumination that is much easier on the eyes when reading in the daytime. And while document storage is perhaps less of an issue than it once was, make sure that you have plenty of room for filing and equipment, ideally custom-built to make the most of all the available space. There is no reason why this needs to look functional or corporate; a bespoke design in a striking color will complement any room beautifully.

A REGENCY TOWN HOUSE IN BATH

OPPOSITE The high ceiling in this elegant study provided an opportunity to fit extensive storage for books and files while still leaving space for a sofa. **ABOVE** The ladder is designed to hook over a pole running the length of the bookcase and offers secure, convenient access to storage, however high.

WORKING

OPPOSITE While this room accommodates an office area (*above*) with all necessary resources, the remainder of the space functions as a sitting room. **ABOVE** Storage and workspace have been incorporated into the corner of the room with bookcases, drawers, and room for hanging files. Wall lights fitted on either side of the desk create discreet task lighting.

WORKING

A CONTEMPORARY TOWN HOUSE IN KNIGHTSBRIDGE

The floor-to-ceiling custom cabinetry accommodates shelves for books and cupboards for additional storage. It has a pared-back, contemporary feel and a sliding ladder for easy access.

A VICTORIAN TERRACE HOUSE IN PARSONS GREEN

In Emma and John's London residence, a wall of the dining room has been devoted to cupboards and shelves so that the space can be used as an occasional home office.

AN ANCESTRAL HOME IN NORTH YORKSHIRE

OPPOSITE This scheme demonstrates that a study can be comfortable, elegant, and functional. The highly distinctive antique desk sets the tone for the room, along with other pieces including a globe and an equestrian painting. **ABOVE** The glazing of the bookshelf doors protects a collection of antique books from dust.

A LAKESIDE HOUSE IN SURREY

ABOVE An elegant desk with easy access to books and file storage will transform the corner of any room into a home office. **RIGHT** This traditional study has the benefit of extensive garden views. **OVERLEAF** If space allows, a home office is also the perfect location for a cozy seating arrangement. Here, woolen upholstery creates a cosseting feel.

8. Organizing & Maintaining

Practical spaces are key to any beautiful house. A pantry in the kitchen or a cupboard in the hall allows the spaces they serve to be unburdened of things that might be used only occasionally. Or it could be a fully functioning mudroom, flower room, or laundry room that plays a supporting role to other parts of the house. However practical these spaces might be, I am a firm believer that they can be calm, attractive areas where everything has a place and activities such as sorting, washing, ironing, or caring for pets become a pleasure rather than a chore. Depending on the layout of a house—or the needs of a client—we tend to distribute all these types of functions across different spaces. Some might choose to have a laundry room upstairs close to the bedrooms; others will prefer to combine it with a utility room near the kitchen.

In a laundry room, a drying rack suspended from the ceiling, ideally over a table for folding, is a great addition. It also makes sense to utilize all the available space by installing tall cabinets, one of which can accommodate a dryer on top of a washing machine if necessary. Storage that is out of reach can easily be accessed by steps or a ladder. Custom solutions dedicated to specific items, such as laundry baskets or cleaning equipment, are a huge advantage.

If there is sufficient space, a dedicated mudroom could have bespoke storage for shoes, coats, and sports equipment, with receptacles for items that need cleaning. The earlier in the process that you plan storage, the more opportunities you'll have to create spaces for specific items. A locker or shelf and hook for each member of the family makes storing and finding things easier. A mix of open storage (for footwear) and cupboards (for equipment and tools) offers the best of both worlds. Wicker baskets are another practical and aesthetic option.

In laundry areas and mudrooms, a deep sink is the ideal option for soaking and scrubbing. Choose natural surfaces for floors; they look great and are more functional, and materials such as stone and brick combine well with underfloor heating. An eggshell paint is the best for walls, because it is by far the easiest finish to keep clean. Alternatively, paneling can be a smart decision, particularly in a mudroom where dirt is inevitable.

A CONTEMPORARY TOWN HOUSE IN KNIGHTSBRIDGE

OPPOSITE The basement entrance of this town house leads to a lobby area that has been fitted with storage for outdoor clothing and an easily maintained limestone floor. A mirror panel has been fitted to the back of the door. **ABOVE** A utility room provides space for doing laundry and preparing flowers.

ORGANIZING & MAINTAINING

A LAKESIDE HOUSE IN SURREY

OPPOSITE This upstairs laundry room is situated close to family bedrooms, providing a convenient place for drying and ironing clothes away from high-traffic areas downstairs. **ABOVE** Woven storage baskets bring a rustic feel to this mudroom, fitted with a bench seat for putting on and removing boots and shoes.

ORGANIZING & MAINTAINING

A CONVERTED BARN IN WILTSHIRE

Even narrow spaces lend themselves to use as utility rooms. Here, brickwork paving and simple paneling add a pleasing, rustic feel to a laundry area.

A VICTORIAN TERRACE HOUSE IN PARSONS GREEN

In this utility room, patterned floor tiles add a splash of color to the otherwise neutral scheme. In smaller rooms, the addition of a mirror will always enhance the feeling of space.

AN ANCESTRAL HOME IN NORTH YORKSHIRE

In this mudroom, a central table offers a useful place for preparing and checking equipment before and after sporting activities. A large antler chandelier with feather-covered shades was selected in homage to the house's country setting.

230   ORGANIZING & MAINTAINING

ABOVE This small pantry benefits from a glass door and has open shelving that provides easy access to supplies. **OPPOSITE** A traditional butler's sink is the ideal choice for service areas, because it has generous proportions ideally suited to washing large items such as pans and outdoor equipment.

OPPOSITE A double-sided rack significantly increases the amount of storage for coats and boots in this mudroom. With copper hot-water pipes positioned at its center, it was designed to be a drying rack for wet coats after outdoor sports. High shelves at the room's perimeter offer a good option for long-term storage or for the display of interesting collections. **ABOVE** The space also includes floor-to-ceiling hanging storage, cabinetry, and a butler's sink.

A FORMER SCHOOLHOUSE IN OXFORDSHIRE

ABOVE A utility space with pale gray cabinetry, large subway tiles, and paneling to the ceiling has a crisp, contemporary feel. **OPPOSITE** If there isn't space for a dedicated mudroom, a bench beneath a row of coat hooks near a back door keeps outdoor clothing in one place.

A SEASIDE COTTAGE IN CORNWALL

ABOVE With a combination of careful planning and bespoke storage, even the smallest spaces can accommodate a wide range of clothing. **OPPOSITE** This small, glass-paneled extension, which leads to the garden, not only makes the most of the garden views but also provides storage space in the recesses on both sides of the door.

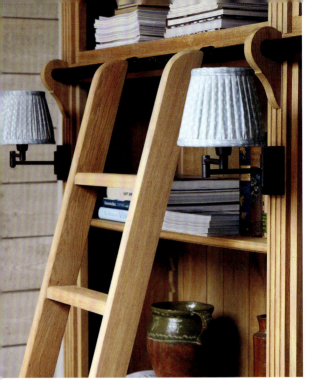

Sims Hilditch Design Studio

Behind each and every one of the projects in this book is the Sims Hilditch team who works creatively and collaboratively at our studio in the countryside near Bath. Our office takes its name from The White Hart, a sixteenth-century building that began life as a coaching inn. Despite its historic status, when we took it on almost a decade ago it was derelict and required a complete restoration; it needed gutting and a thorough reimagination of the layout and spatial planning in order to bring it into the twenty-first century.

We were keen to work in spaces designed to the same standard as those we create for clients, and to have interiors that would act as a showcase for what Sims Hilditch can achieve. The challenge for our design team was conceiving a contemporary studio that was also rooted in a traditional country style that met the demands of the building's listed status. Luckily, many of the inn's original features were still intact, such as the Cotswold stone walls and the beautiful wood beams that support its pitched roof. We were careful to retain these features by sympathetically incorporating them into the design.

Our interiors are often inspired by nature, so the rolling fields and open skies surrounding the studio called for creating a welcoming country aesthetic filled with natural light. We installed glazed steel doors to allow privacy without compromising the ambient light, and we retained the exposed beams and stone walls in the kitchen to keep the building rooted in its country heritage.

We are known for our new English style with a twist, and the way we styled the interior echoes this. We paired contemporary and traditional pieces and placed emphasis on natural materials and textures. We were careful not to select anything "on trend" to ensure that the design remained elegant and timeless. An open-plan layout further facilitated an inviting and collaborative workspace. So while we split the ground floor into dedicated zones for design work, meetings, eating, and entertaining, we installed internal doors sparingly to preserve a sense of cohesion and flow from room to room. This approach maintains a sense of structure that supports the overall aesthetic, making this a pleasing environment in which to work.

OPPOSITE Crisp, contemporary design including lighting, cabinetry, and upholstery has been employed to transform the derelict coaching inn into a comfortable and efficient space.
OVERLEAF Shiplap-lined walls, bespoke storage, and a skylight combine to create a look that epitomizes the possibilities offered by the Sims Hilditch studio.

OPPOSITE Limestone floors, natural light, exposed lime-washed beams, and oak furniture create a light, airy feel not normally associated with buildings of this period. **ABOVE** As in Emma's residential projects, antiques lend texture and mood to the space and mix seamlessly with contemporary pieces.

OPPOSITE A soft-orange color creates a vibrant space to work. Bespoke cabinetry offers plenty of storage for plans and samples as well as space for meetings. **ABOVE** Steel doors and partitions offer an opportunity to divide the space while ensuring that it benefits from all available natural light.

ABOVE The simplicity of bespoke cabinetry offers a crisp but complementary contrast to the rugged appearance of the local limestone. OPPOSITE Contemporary joinery and an inviting bench are part of a perfectly functioning cooking and dining space in unlikely surroundings. The lofty ceiling adds drama to the setting.

ABOVE Although these are commercial premises, Emma believes passionately in the importance of cultivating vegetables and flowers as a way of enhancing the quality of everyday life. **RIGHT** A terrace was designed for outdoor meals and client meetings. **OVERLEAF** The exterior of the old coaching inn has been transformed to meet the demands of the twenty-first century.

Acknowledgments

I gratefully acknowledge the contributions of the following people:

Our clients, who have made it all possible, for their trust and kindness. They are my greatest collaborators, and I'm eternally grateful to them for choosing Sims Hilditch.

Giles Kime, for his ongoing support and friendship. His words have brought my work to life.

Philip Reeser, my editor at Rizzoli, who has been the source of fantastic guidance.

Kit Kemp for writing the foreword. I admired her long before she became a friend.

Naomi Glynn, who managed the creation of the book's content and was the driving force behind the photographic shoots.

Simon Brown, who brought his considerable flair and expertise to the photography.

Kasia Turek and Hana Snow for styling the photography.

Celia Fuller, who has worked her magic on the design of this beautiful book.

My supremely talented team without whom these projects would not be possible.

Joanna Binder, my right-hand woman and Sims Hilditch's managing director, for her constant positivity and friendship.

My husband, John, for all his support.

And finally, my parents for giving me the most wonderful creative upbringing.

Emma Sims-Hilditch

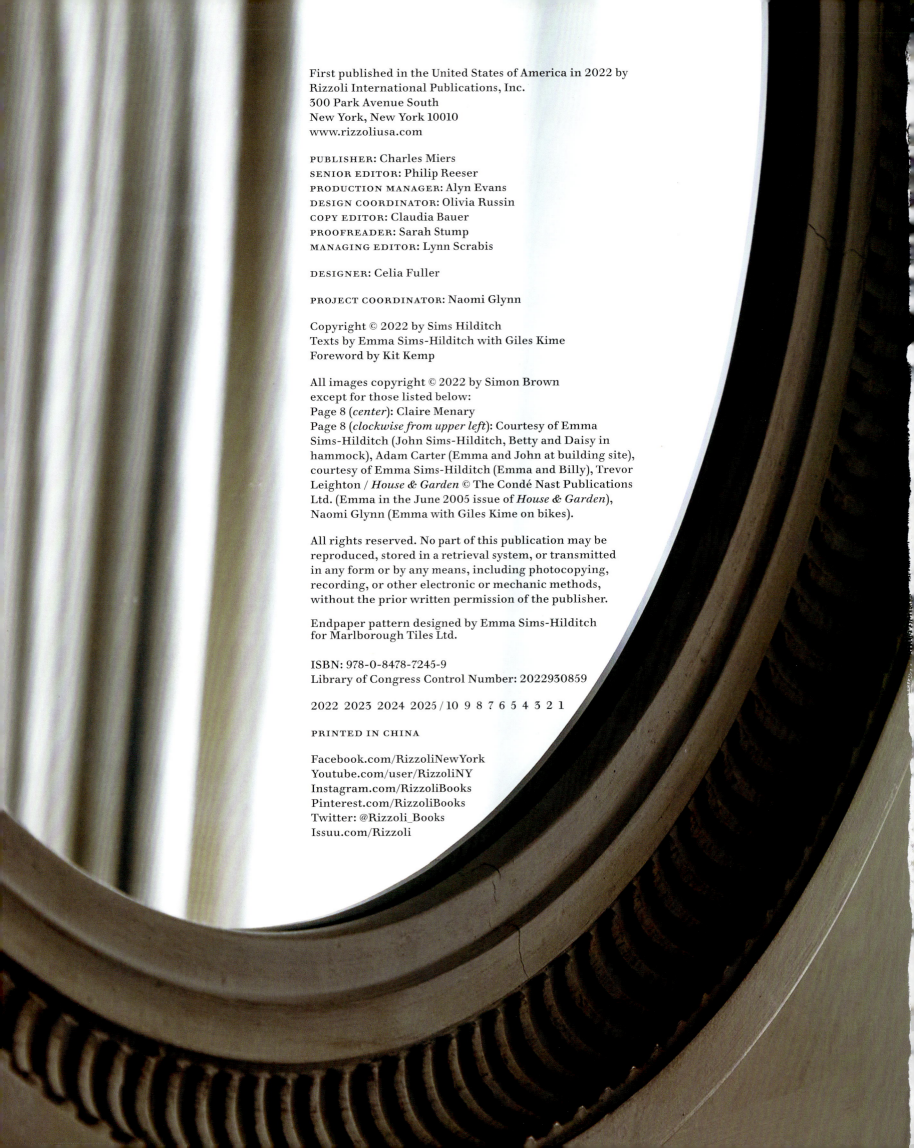

First published in the United States of America in 2022 by
Rizzoli International Publications, Inc.
300 Park Avenue South
New York, New York 10010
www.rizzoliusa.com

PUBLISHER: Charles Miers
SENIOR EDITOR: Philip Reeser
PRODUCTION MANAGER: Alyn Evans
DESIGN COORDINATOR: Olivia Russin
COPY EDITOR: Claudia Bauer
PROOFREADER: Sarah Stump
MANAGING EDITOR: Lynn Scrabis

DESIGNER: Celia Fuller

PROJECT COORDINATOR: Naomi Glynn

Copyright © 2022 by Sims Hilditch
Texts by Emma Sims-Hilditch with Giles Kime
Foreword by Kit Kemp

All images copyright © 2022 by Simon Brown
except for those listed below:
Page 8 (*center*): Claire Menary
Page 8 (*clockwise from upper left*): Courtesy of Emma Sims-Hilditch (John Sims-Hilditch, Betty and Daisy in hammock), Adam Carter (Emma and John at building site), courtesy of Emma Sims-Hilditch (Emma and Billy), Trevor Leighton / *House & Garden* © The Condé Nast Publications Ltd. (Emma in the June 2005 issue of *House & Garden*), Naomi Glynn (Emma with Giles Kime on bikes).

All rights reserved. No part of this publication may be reproduced, stored in a retrieval system, or transmitted in any form or by any means, including photocopying, recording, or other electronic or mechanic methods, without the prior written permission of the publisher.

Endpaper pattern designed by Emma Sims-Hilditch for Marlborough Tiles Ltd.

ISBN: 978-0-8478-7245-9
Library of Congress Control Number: 2022930859

2022 2023 2024 2025 / 10 9 8 7 6 5 4 3 2 1

PRINTED IN CHINA

Facebook.com/RizzoliNewYork
Youtube.com/user/RizzoliNY
Instagram.com/RizzoliBooks
Pinterest.com/RizzoliBooks
Twitter: @Rizzoli_Books
Issuu.com/Rizzoli